The Uncorrected World

The Wesleyan Poetry Program: Volume 67

The
Uncorrected
World

by

Kenneth O. Hanson

Wesleyan University Press

Middletown, Connecticut

Acknowledgement is gratefully made to *Poetry Northwest,* in the pages of which many of the poems in this book were first published, and to the other periodical journals following: *The Iowa Review, Ironwood, kayak, Lillabulero, The Nation* and *Ophir.*
    Some of these poems first appeared in a limited-edition chapbook entitled *Saronikos and Other Poems,* published by Press-22 of Portland, Oregon, in 1970.

Library of Congress Cataloging in Publication Data

Hanson, Kenneth O   1922–
    The uncorrected world.

    (The Wesleyan poetry program, v. 67)
    Poems.
    I. Title.
PS3558.A52U5   811'.5'4   73–6012
ISBN 0–8195–2067–5
ISBN 0–8195–1067–X (pbk.)

811.54
H19u

Manufactured in the United States of America
First edition

Contents

The Uncorrected World

On Time

The Athenian summer
has come down from the mountains.
Its random histories
exhaust themselves on the beaches.
Fragments of sentences.
Was there ever
any other kind of weather?

Saronikos

9 a.m. in a hot sun
and the waiter Plato
hasn't come. At ten
he brings me Amstel
rolls down the awning
sweeps last night's fish bones
onto the beach.
I read in *The Athens News*
another Greek has got his ear
bit off in a taverna
in a quarrel over
who pays the tab.
The Greek fuzz found it
under the table. Nobody
sewed it back. I look
at Plato closely. Both
ears are in place. It's
early in the day but late
in life. Across the bay
the white cruise ship
is sailing to the islands.
Here I'm turning
browner than a berry.
Months to go. I touch
both ears. At two o'clock
I pay the tab.

After the April Coup

Beginning the day with ouzo
you're one jump ahead.
I stick to beer.
Together we read *The Athens News.*
Today they're banning
the breaking of plates for fun.
A painter from Vancouver says
he's selling his tape recorder
since "you can't hold music."
O god has made the world he cries.
Out there the world
is taking some damned odd turns.
I try to give in until
I think of Sancho Panza saying
I am surrendered enough already.
Here on my island, under
the blue umbrellas, birds
fly off in all directions.
Mary who brought champagne
has gone to Spain to look at Goyas.
Duncan, a spiritual presence
goes to look at brothels.
God is on our side the government says.
And Costa is growing a beard
to look more serious
as the day is making its slow way
toward the Capri Bar, Elena and John
and a night with the planets
still in their orbits.

After The Countercoup That Failed

O king in exile!
O inconstant king!
What will the fishermen in Kalamáki
left to the colonels do
when the colonels disapprove
of conversational get-
togethers, drinking and dancing
and the breaking of plates for fun?
How in the grip
of hot-syllabled political passion
can you insult the king
when there is no king?
What will the fishermen in Kalamáki
do but spread their nets
as yellow as the sun
beside the sea, blue as the sky
and name the colonels one by one
until the colonels' names
turn bitter on the tongue?

Political Poem

If it looks like a poppy, it is a poppy.
— Nikos Tselepides

Prices are up
twenty per cent for the week
and the Greeks are
singing together for Easter.

A band of the blind
is playing 'Roll Out the Barrels'
and moving like bats by radar
around Syntagma Square
while friends with locked cannisters
are collecting coins
to pay for the coming
season of the Attic sun.

Babis who went last week
with a Greek doctor
"and we didn't sleep all the night"
is now going with a German
tourist for money.
I am irregular he says
like Cavafy but I don't know why
I can't do it except for money.

From a sidewalk cafe
a Greek, watching a Greek
woman pass, tells her critically
You walk like the political situation.

On all the busy
corners of Athens, police
whistles are shrilling
like the first cicadas.
Now in spite of censorship
Greeks by the sea
or sitting on stones
are flexing their muscles
and dreaming of a new Marathon.

Easter 1969

Riding the good road
built by NATO, out
of Athens to Levádia
Paris and Helen in
the back seat picked their
mountain flowers paid
respect to powerlines
and altogether scamped
the roast lambs trussed
on village spits, blue
smoke in all directions
while the season turned.
O brave new world
to wind up by the road
in something four-square white
the floor scrubbed clean
a skinned lamb hanging
by the heels in center room
beyond which looking tough
tacked on the wall beside
the king and queen in exile
Papadopoulos and Pattakós
pinpoint the day.
A Christian nation one
not yet quite ready for
democracy the papers say
two thousand years after
they first made up the word.
A dragged out beaten cur
three legs is hanging round
the door as I pay the bill
my heart not in it

and we make our way back out
into anonymous sunlight.
The driver's got some
friends we visit ten
miles up some goat trail
and the locked church suddenly
is opened, built
on top a spring whose water
dipped in a tin cup
grates the teeth. Askrá
they tell me here's Askrá
birthplace of Hesiod
surprised I know him.
Then they photograph the spot
themselves in various
combinations by the church
Paris and Helen, Evangelos
and Helen, Helen and Anthoúla
Paris and Evangelos. I
take my turn. The vast
light breaks the ages down
damned cold in winter damned
hot in summer. How
could he.love this land
outpost of nowhere
murderous as myth.
Sun up, to work. Sun
down, to rest. This rocky
landscape Hesiod how could he

plow a straight furrow?
Three thousand years.
Sun. Moon. Stone. Sky.
Against the whitewashed wall.
Official pronouncements.

Athens in August

Behind the 19th-century Parliament Building
hangs a 19th-century sky, too pink
and baby blue at sunset for my taste.

The cats beneath the orange trees
fed once by one who brought them scraps
wrapped in the fishy news

have gone elsewhere. The government I think
refused to take them seriously.
Greece for the Christian Greeks

they advertise, between
the Coca-Cola signs. Armed soldiers
rise in flames along Syngrou

and on the postage stamps. The sun
takes no account in August
and burns everything to a crisp.

It rolls through the atmosphere
like money. Near the park
that was the king's, a villager

from Thessaly plays the flute. Some
peacocks shift in dusty pens. The soldiers
and their girls walk by in pairs

urgent as history.

The Sixth Fleet Is In

The sunlight glitters on the bay.
The American sailors walk in schools
like fish, with cameras
and transistor radios.
Their God is watching them.
He knows all and it saddens him.
They sparkle in their
innocence and whites
but they are anxious to sin
and waiting to be taken in.
And Greeks oblige
and this is nothing new.
Their God is older and he smiles.
In hundreds of tavernas
paramýthy flows, in praise
of ingenuity. In suburbs some
19 year old Helen is always doing it.
The sunlight glitters on the bay
and in their blood
the Greeks know life is good
today is today, and everywhere
the hilarious face of God.

On the Square — Syntagma

John
who called his club Imperial
'because that means the best'
then did it up in knotty pine
puts on his cards "A floor show nightly
featuring the internationally famous
Imperial striptease girls"
— there is no floor show
and there are no striptease girls.
The booze is watered
and the doorman queer.
John is incapable of blushing
and his card concludes
"One visit will persuade you."

Capri Bar

No room to turn around
three girls behind the bar
fat owner ageless
here you are
why should you turn around
in August
the electric fan
surveys the room
not making much difference
Venus Anadyomene
have a heart
it's August
the regulars
have all been here
two thousand years
they know the score
they knew the score
long before Alexander
the northerner
there's more
than one way to conquer
so you build a city
take them in
Alexandria or Thebes
you build a lighthouse
keep to yourself
or pretend to speak
their foreign language
barbarous and now
they say blind Homer
'knew hieroglyphics'
barbarous and what's the use

sooner or later
it all comes home
the Parthenon one
great boondoggle
so the Arabs come
tough customers
the jukebox changes
and the balance shifts
but sooner or later
here comes the same
old song again
"you can't keep two
big oranges in one
pocket" can't
you now

Maria

She was kept in a small apartment
by a fancy man, who used to see her
twice a week. I'd hear them singing
through the wall. I thought they were married.
But then the singing stopped. The fancy man
no longer came. It was quiet as hell
all afternoon. And one day four
very tall policemen carried her out
like a sack of wheat, in the sling of a blanket
stark naked, and the color of suet.
I never learned her proper name.
Nobody wondered why she did it.

Bouzouki

Listening to rock 'n roll
on the American Armed
Forces radio station in Athens
Evangelos says Americans
are crazy and changes the station
to bouzouki where the voice
of Kazantzides makes its way
despairing through a world
of broken promises, anonymous
letters and the basic Greek emotions.
This is the music to break
plates to. It simply leaves
no stone unturned.
Every day a new landscape
and the heart, peeled like an onion.

Thermoplyae

The blind bird sings
one note or a series

The sun like a schoolboy
leans in the doorway

What are they doing
there on the border

the lost syllables
like gun emplacements

Tsiganos

He picks up a stone
to sharpen his knife.
There is nothing, no one
under the stone.
The sun is furious
and circles him slowly
like an opponent.
It holds the future
thin as a knife blade
blind as the verb to be.
It falls on the knife
and the blade wastes
sharpened on stone.
All the fish in the bay
are two thousand years old.
Why does it suddenly
have to be me?

Edem

Down the stone steps
regular as the weather
every day at one, the two
came, the young one
carrying the other, old
enough to be his father
over his shoulder
like a bundle of sticks
and put him down on
a blanket over the rocks,
and stripped to their shorts
for an hour, both
faced a sun ferocious
enough to peel paint
from a fender, and
looked at the level sea
where almost nothing
sailed by, and if it did
it wasn't for them
just part of the weather.
Kids kicked beach balls
soccer-style around them
scattering sand, and
swimmers in shallow water
cried Thalassa! Thalassa!
not to each other
but to the sea, as if
it needed reminding.
Now and then the young
one rearranged his father
on the stones, one

arrangement, then another
imperfect, then slung him
over his shoulder, back
up the stone steps
dazzling with mica
like walking on stars
to the life they had come from
perhaps a balcony
perhaps a garden.

Cinema

Overnight
a new week has come
to the walls of Athens.
Workmen with bikes
and buckets of paste
have spent all night
changing the face of the city.
Two lovers, repeating
themselves for miles
smile vacantly
exclusively at each other
ignoring the wishful
thinking of the passengers
on buses. Love, love
the blind man sings
by the Popular Bank
knowing nothing has changed
but the signs.

Short Story

When he first
met her he stood
stockstill — the cars
backed up for
blocks, all honking
to beat the band.
That was Tuesday.
Already he wonders
how much longer
he can bear that
regular traffic
her eyes her lips
her tongue her hair

The Durable

It is said
things speak for themselves.
The faint cicadas sing
like Paganini in the fig tree next door.
The fragment moon like a decayed molar
smiles at the coming
and going of the sea. The Greek
streetcleaner smiles at me.
Oranges. We speak the same language.
And there are no witnesses.

Greek Wedding

Remembering now, later
September
that brilliant weather
sun in the million
miles of sky
ringing like churchbells

that once in a lifetime
stretching forever
Anthoúla, pretty as a picture
crowned with flowers
plastic forever

Evangelos, movie star
for the moment
captured on film by
the paid photographer
the black priest muttering
details of the moment

recorded by cameras
except
that moment later
footsteps
stopped, the white
apartment, second
floor, and the green bed
covered with money

Man Singing Bouzouki

He is married.
She is beautiful.
They are happy.
He is alone
on his motorcycle.
He sings into the wind.
His throat is tight.
The cars stream past.
He listens to himself.
She is unfaithful.
I tear my clothes.
I gave her everything.
Why did she leave me
for another man?

Desperate Moves

They say the chameleon
has no character.
He takes his color
from the wall — a red
shadow, green leaf
whatever comes to hand.
What do they know
of the close connections
that go into his
split-second timing.
There are those who neither
see him coming nor going.

Greeks Being Happy

It is not something you are.
It is something you do.
It is not your own private affair.
All the world says Bravo!
It is a Greek at bouzouki
so drunk he can't stand
one friend on each side
holding him up so he can dance.
It is everyone watching sober
being happy with him.

Late November

—still, no rain in Athens.
Bishops and priests have had
ceremonies and prayed for it.

There have been 10-minute
electricity blackouts
and the company says

it's because the wires
"haven't been washed by rain"
which is hard to believe.

But the country is Christian
in a sane sort of way, and the priests
carry on with their praying

whether it rains or not.
Meanwhile, the sun is out—
good reason for a give and take

whatever the company says.
I remember once a year ago
in Turkey, some farmers in arms

threw rocks at the American Embassy
to protest 'the holes in the sky'
American missiles made

which let their rains come down, too much.
I guess it doesn't work in Greece.
There's always Zeus, but then

there's always Pan, waiting in the wings.
These things are real
in spite of what the company says.

Tomorrow, who knows?

In This Square Room

I listen to a round rain
falling on the anarchic trees.
A car or two is stitching
its mechanical progress
up the hill. The wheels
sound like zippers being
opened. Athens I hear
has put up a papier-maché
figure of a discus-thrower
in Syntagma Square
assembled slowly from
the ground floor up —
the thighs, the crotch
a flying penis pointing
toward American Express
and there it stayed
three days exciting
tourists to photography
Greek women to their private jokes
and men to say it's time
they put a prick on a pedestal
in Constitution Square —
three days and then
the project was complete
the head the torso and the disc
the whole thing painted bronze
three other copies
in the squares in town —
and slowly slowly
rain came down.
The orange trees

in Athens keep their care.
The slow cars zipper up the street.
September 5, winter began.

Nick with the News

tells me the statue
has been taken down

    Snyder's SAND
from the desert?
      —when will be sand again.
Compare.
    Kazantzakis'
My sun, great easterner
    my Oriental one?
Anatolite
    "from the east."

    Saronikos—
Asia Oceania America etc.
'Still there are
    many tourists'—
technicians
    of the sacred.
I see your point.
The statue
    has been torn down.
Paul the waiter
    Panos the crazy kid
send greetings.
    Solitary trees—
where are we now Dimitrios?

On the border
    lusting after
both sides of it
    still Greek.

Poem on History

Ibn Saud is dead
and the gods in his head
are all dead too
who lived by oil
as his sons by scotch
and paid thirty thousand
a month all told
to live in a villa
on the beach near Voula

Gone are the wives and
the princes the fleet
of cadillacs and the two
bodyguards who held him up
but if the Greek
government is grieved
the landscape is unmoved
there have been kings before
and more than enough
to go around

"Scentless, colorless,
solitary, rock-loving—memory
is all of these"—echoes
that die in the trees
gypsies with performing
monkeys beating
tambourines great
beetles tied on strings for sale
beside the fish-rich sea
beside this un-
changed curve of bay

Flisvos Bus-stop

On a summer day
they crossed the square
a man a woman and two children
and sat at a zinc topped table
under the witness trees
a young man with a thick moustache
almost Albanian composed
as the Greeks can be
who know the leaves fall gently
in fine weather
a thin woman and two children
who circled the table
and he sat one hand
in his lap the other
on the zinc topped table
both hands in black gloves
the fingers curved
and when the coffee came
the woman lifted the cup to his lips
and set it down again
and put a cigarette
into his mouth and lighted that
and took it out to knock the ash off
and finished her coffee
and nagged at the children
and took his coin purse
out of his jacket pocket
and put the drachmas
on the zinc topped table
and put the coin purse
back into his pocket
and took the cigarette from his mouth

42

and put it out on the zinc topped table
and the man smiled
and they walked off
with the children
his two hands in their black gloves
curved the same way
swinging at his sides
and on the zinc topped table
a leaf fell
into the half-full coffee cup
and the waiter came
and picked the drachmas up
and took the coffee cups away
and wiped the zinc topped table clean

Areos 3 on a Name Day

In the fall, a Greek
friend wrote, 'In the fall
who can count the Greeks
and come up with a round number?'
Now it is March.
A light rain is falling
and he writes about
an old poet muttering
which is better, blood or wine?

In a Greek bar, music on tape
is playing in four languages
none of them Greek.
There are eight
American warships in the Bay
for Greek Independence Day.
Three days ago, before parades
the Alien Police
to fill out a form asked me
Do you have any money?
and What do you believe?

I believe in retsina.
I also believe
in the *mikró* at Vassili's
who looks like a painting by Soutine.
I believe in the honey
of Mount Hymettus. I believe
in the wisdom of Kung
(Things have their roots
and branches) and I
believe in the world of Evangelos.

44

This is his day. He comes
from Kallithéa like *meltémi*
on his motorbike.
We play *koun-kan*.
Uncles and aunts and cousins wait.
He holds two jokers
and he says I cheat.
Bouzouki falls from all the ceiling
and the walls. I drink to Greece
his name day and the Greeks
and write his name
this name day in a book, carefully
as if I might forget.

Next

One night in a bad mood
alone in a foreign city
merákia or worse
a black mood, I went
by cab to find a friend
six times he was not home
the neighbors had me in for drinks
assuring me he will be here
the taxi driver thinking
drunk crazy American
not *merákia* or worse
and the last time I found him
home, in bed with his wife
who spoke no English but
made me a cup of strong Greek coffee
while I wept by the bed
merákia or worse and
he assured me his house was my house
and in the world I had one friend
went home by cab to bounce
off the walls and finally
to fall in my bed alone
dreaming of conveyor belts and pulleys
and all those moving parts
in which I only
gum up the works
and woke to a Greek morning
rigid and at attention
neither saved nor damned
neither dead nor alive
wondering what next

Near Skala (Peloponnese)

Looking for ruins
we took our time.
The villagers, who
had lived there for years
always pointed up
though I do not know
if they knew what a ruin was.
When we got to the top
there was only a pile
of stones, looking much
like the other stones. Was this
a ruin? It wasn't what
I had been led to expect
from novels and old engravings.
No two stones formed a pattern
and it was hard to imagine
anyone living there long
in anything like grandeur.

Well, here we are
the guide said indifferent.
Not quite what I asked for
I thought feigning interest.
We'd come a long way
and I didn't want him
disgruntled. The way down
we passed loaded olive trucks
parked on a road only
wide as their truckbed.
How we inched by, two wheels
hanging over the valley
I'll never know. I thought

47

we were goners more than once.
Still, the breeze was refreshing
the view of the valley
like something in plastic
the air was that palpable.

And on the way down
after passing the trucks
we drank from a spring
guaranteed to make you
immortal. This was not
in the guidebooks. I learned
only later, a thousand
such springs in the country
will do the same, each one
with its own history.

You will forget, but
you will live forever
the guide said confidently.
What good is that I thought
if there's nothing to remember.
But I drank anyway.
The water was cold and
tasted of stones. It was
not sweet, it was somehow
more real than that
and reminded me both
of the mountain and of the valley.
I can taste it still
so that part at least
of the story was false.

As for the rest, it's best
not to think too far ahead.
Later I drank from some
of the other springs, which
I found rather disappointing.
I think, looking back now
only the first one counts.

Thinking It Through

I tell you, off the record
Propertius, pissed (III, xxi)
put down, "I must set out
for Athens, home of wisdom —
Athens may break my bonds
at last." But this he thought
could be done with honor
leaving him free to die
as the Greeks do, reconciled
and not like a man divided
cut in two by love, split
down the middle and discarded
like a squeezed lemon. Alas
in the act it proved otherwise.
That's always how it is
with the high dream — something
melts the wax from your wings.
When he got to Athens it was
the prime season, the hotel
rooms booked by rich disappointed
lovers from the East, Arabs
and others. So he took a small
house near the beach, talking
not as he had imagined, to
philosophers like Epicurus
but to the streetcleaner
and the shrewish landlady.
It was a hard life — nobody
cared to hear *his* story.
When he decided to go back
to Rome, he had other things

on his mind than Cynthia
and deep in debt skipped town
on a dark night. When
he docked he had nothing to
declare but his skin (he was
all in one piece) and his store
of Athenian wisdom — just
what he went for. It was
all in his head, chitchat
and mountain melodies, his heart
as light as his purse.
As for Cynthia, once back
it was just the same as before.
Nothing had changed. He was
trained dog and doormat, and
everything went down on paper.

End of the Month Report

I have washed the windows
I have signed the checks
I have arranged the books
according to the six principles
in my head
I have found my poems
in a new anthology
cheek by jowl
with Robert Lowell
I have taken this into account
I have bought the beer for today
I have reread the material
on the Industrial Revolution for Monday
I have read the student papers
I am pledged to read
I have put my life in order
Why then do the bits and pieces
of another landscape
fragments of a great despair
gather in a sidestreet
with obscene gestures
chanting fuck your order
long live doubt
long live the *paramýthy* of the heart
the storm and stress
of the bounced check
the pure disinclination
of the who knows what
the shipwreck always
of the uncertainty at the door
long live the domestic
tranquility of chaos

the rocks and water
of negative capability
the raw discrimination
of the checks and balances
O burn the papers, put the books
again in the damp basement
Christopher Smart molding
alongside the Cat Man of Katmandu
cheek by jowl with Lady Winchilsea
O to be merely clever
like the students of Salonika
who believe in nothing but themselves
or their uncles, which in this case
is something to believe in
O to have antecedents
without thinking them up
to have only
lies to contend with
the indiscriminate sun
in a plastic bag and the yellow wine
more clear than a washed window
week in and week out

In March

I look at the bright outside
through a grimy window.
Sure enough it is not the blue
Aegean. Light on the leaves
lies thin as skim milk.
It turns the stomach.
Nothing else is moving, except
perhaps the Swedish gardener
who comes and goes next door
with his power mower
and who last year trimmed my hedges
to improve the neighborhood
though I hadn't asked.
I wish him luck, through a
grimy window, luck with
the skim milk too, jays
in the trees, the few
azaleas, black bamboo. Always
remember you are an American
I'm advised. Sure enough
this is not the blue Aegean.
I pledge allegiance, cross my heart
as the neighborhood Indians
come out of their reservations
nothing to fear. The Swedish
gardener goes back to his suburb
leaving only the pollution haze
index. The roses are intact.

He has his own reservations
American through and through
and I wonder what was the matter
with last year, why is the blue
Aegean blue?

First of All

First of all it is necessary
to find yourself a country
—which is not easy.
It takes much looking
after which you must be lucky.
There must be rocks and water
and a sky that is willing
to take itself for granted
without being overbearing.
There should be fresh fish
in the harbor, fresh bread
in the local stores.
The people should know
how to suffer without
being unhappy, and how to be happy
without feeling guilty. The men
should be named Dimitrios
Costa, John or Evangelos
and all the women should be
named Elena or Anthoúla.
The newspapers should always
lie, which gives you something
to think about. There should be
great gods in the background
and on all the mountain tops.
There should be lesser gods
in the fields, and nymphs
about all the cool fountains.
The past should be always
somewhere in the distance,
not taken too seriously
but there always giving perspective.

The present should consist of the seven
days of the week forever.
The music should be broken-hearted
without being self-indulgent.
It should be difficult to sing.
Even the birds in the trees should
work for a dangerous living.
When it rains there should be
no doubt about it. The people
should be hard to govern
and not know how to queue up.
They should come from the villages
and go out to sea, and go back
to the villages. There should be
no word in their language
for self-pity. They should be
farmers and sailors, with only
a few poets. The olive trees
and the orange trees and the cypress
will change your life, the rocks
and the lies and the gods
and the strict music. If you go there
you should be prepared to leave
at a moment's notice, knowing
after all you have been somewhere.

O Distances We Gaze Into

This afternoon too comfortable on Carlton St.
I think of those adventurers
who ate sheep's eyeballs, entrails

rancid butter and the brains of monkeys
while too chicken-hearted
I stayed home and read Herodotus

the Abbe Huc on Tartary
the X Bar X Boys at Grizzly Pass
and Han Yü speaking to the crocodile.

I've filled the house three times today
with bouzouki, hoping to call back
the sparrows at Papaspirou's

open skies and open hearts and open palms
Plaka, Angelopolous and Kazantzides—
nothing compels the mind like music.

Madly the sun dances on the water
on chips of broken bottles, glass and some obsidian
and I'm reminded of Fort Hall

where years ago some rundown Indians in dust
danced days and nights around a center pole
to shuffling drums and chant.

What changes is the view.
Let's say the traveler anywhere wants
a vista a prospect a view.

Goose Bay, Goose Prairie, Mt. St. Joy
the lion's out, contagion's in the air.
Travelers urged by the sun, seeking

its farthest reaches, travelers
putting the miles between themselves
and Tombstone by nightfall

travelers ransacking private alphabets
to name their histories letter by letter—
Here I am at Angkor Wat, here I am

by the Bay of Naples. Now I am
putting on my shoe. We face
the force that binds in green variety Pierrot

the plane that sheers the steeple flat
the mild brouhaha on the mossy stones.
We like to seem importunate

before this world of change.
O plains o vasty deep o marge and void
etc. We move but not through distance

into time, as if the fatal toad
in time's thin stone still faintly ticked
somewhere beyond. Aficionados of the moon!

O distances we gaze into!